50 Herbs, Spices and Condiments Recipes for Home

By: Kelly Johnson

Table of Contents

Herbs Recipes:

- Basil Pesto
- Rosemary Roasted Potatoes
- Cilantro-Lime Rice
- Minty Tzatziki
- Thyme-infused Roast Chicken
- Dill Pickle Potato Salad
- Lemon-Herb Grilled Fish
- Chimichurri Sauce
- Mint Chocolate Chip Ice Cream
- Herb-Marinated Grilled Lamb Chops
- Chive and Garlic Mashed Potatoes

Spice Recipes:

- Homemade Garam Masala
- Chili Powder
- Five-Spice Powder
- Smoky Paprika Chicken
- Curry Powder
- Za'atar Roasted Vegetables
- Cajun Shrimp Pasta
- Japanese Shichimi Togarashi Spice Mix
- Turmeric Golden Milk
- Blackened Cajun Salmon
- Chinese Five-Spice Roasted Nuts

Condiments Recipes:

- Homemade Ketchup
- Garlic Aioli
- Salsa Verde
- Honey Mustard Sauce
- Harissa Paste

- Avocado Lime Crema
- Homemade Sriracha Sauce
- Cucumber Raita
- Mango Salsa
- Chutney
- Balsamic Glaze

Specialty Herb and Spice Blends:

- Herbes de Provence
- Ras el Hanout
- Italian Seasoning Blend
- Taco Seasoning Mix
- Adobe Seasoning
- Berbere Spice Blend
- Shawarma Seasoning
- Sesame Ginger Dressing
- Jerk Seasoning
- Greek Souvlaki Marinade
- Moroccan Ras el Hanout Hummus

Homemade Sauces:

- Hollandaise Sauce
- Soy-Ginger Glaze
- Homemade BBQ Sauce
- Teriyaki Glaze
- Homemade Enchilada Sauce
- Sun-Dried Tomato Pesto

Herbs Recipes:

Basil Pesto

Ingredients:

- 2 cups fresh basil leaves, packed
- 1/2 cup grated Parmesan cheese
- 1/2 cup pine nuts, toasted
- 3 cloves garlic
- 1 cup extra-virgin olive oil
- Salt and pepper, to taste

Instructions:

Prepare Basil: Wash and dry the fresh basil leaves, ensuring they are clean and free of excess moisture.

Toast Pine Nuts: In a dry skillet over medium heat, toast the pine nuts until they are lightly golden. Keep a close eye on them as they can burn quickly. Set aside to cool.

Blend Ingredients: In a food processor, combine the basil, grated Parmesan, toasted pine nuts, and garlic cloves. Pulse until the ingredients are finely chopped.

Stream in Olive Oil: With the food processor running, slowly stream in the olive oil. Continue blending until the mixture forms a smooth, well-combined paste.

Season: Season the pesto with salt and pepper to taste. Adjust the seasoning as needed.

Store: Transfer the basil pesto to a jar or airtight container. If not using immediately, you can refrigerate it for a few days or freeze it for longer storage.

Serve: Use the basil pesto as a sauce for pasta, a spread on bread or crackers, a topping for grilled meats or vegetables, or as a flavorful addition to various dishes.

Feel free to adjust the quantities of ingredients based on personal preferences, and enjoy the vibrant flavors of homemade basil pesto!

Rosemary Roasted Potatoes

Ingredients:

- 2 pounds (about 1 kg) baby potatoes, washed and halved
- 3 tablespoons olive oil
- 2 tablespoons fresh rosemary, finely chopped
- 3 cloves garlic, minced
- Salt and pepper, to taste

Instructions:

Preheat Oven: Preheat your oven to 425°F (220°C).
Prepare Potatoes: If the potatoes are larger, you can quarter them. Place the halved or quartered potatoes in a large bowl.
Season Potatoes: Drizzle the potatoes with olive oil, ensuring they are well-coated. Add minced garlic, chopped rosemary, salt, and pepper. Toss the potatoes until evenly coated with the seasonings.
Spread on Baking Sheet: Transfer the seasoned potatoes to a baking sheet, spreading them out in a single layer. This helps them roast evenly.
Roast: Place the baking sheet in the preheated oven and roast for about 25-30 minutes or until the potatoes are golden brown and crispy on the edges. Be sure to toss the potatoes halfway through cooking to ensure even roasting.
Serve: Once the potatoes are roasted to perfection, remove them from the oven. Garnish with additional fresh rosemary if desired and serve immediately.

These Rosemary Roasted Potatoes make a wonderful side dish for various meals. The combination of crispy exteriors and the aromatic flavor of rosemary makes them a delicious addition to any table. Enjoy!

Cilantro-Lime Rice

Ingredients:

- 1 cup long-grain white rice
- 2 cups water
- 1 tablespoon olive oil or butter
- 1 teaspoon salt
- Zest of 1 lime
- 2 tablespoons fresh lime juice
- 1/2 cup fresh cilantro, chopped

Instructions:

Cook Rice: Rinse the rice under cold water until the water runs clear. In a saucepan, combine the rinsed rice, water, olive oil (or butter), and salt. Bring it to a boil.

Simmer: Once boiling, reduce the heat to low, cover, and simmer for 15-20 minutes or until the rice is tender and the water is absorbed.

Fluff Rice: Remove the saucepan from the heat and let it sit, covered, for an additional 5 minutes. Then, fluff the rice with a fork to separate the grains.

Add Lime Zest: While the rice is still warm, add the lime zest. This allows the rice to absorb the citrusy flavors.

Add Lime Juice and Cilantro: Drizzle the fresh lime juice over the rice and add the chopped cilantro. Gently toss the rice with a fork until the lime juice and cilantro are evenly distributed.

Serve: Transfer the Cilantro-Lime Rice to a serving dish and garnish with additional cilantro or lime wedges if desired.

This vibrant and aromatic Cilantro-Lime Rice pairs well with a variety of dishes, especially Mexican or Tex-Mex cuisine. Enjoy!

Minty Tzatziki

Ingredients:

- 1 cup Greek yogurt
- 1/2 cucumber, finely grated and drained
- 2 cloves garlic, minced
- 2 tablespoons fresh mint, finely chopped
- 1 tablespoon fresh dill, finely chopped
- 1 tablespoon extra-virgin olive oil
- 1 tablespoon lemon juice
- Salt and pepper, to taste

Instructions:

Prepare Cucumber: Grate the cucumber and place it in a fine-mesh sieve or cheesecloth over a bowl to drain excess moisture. Press down on the cucumber to remove as much liquid as possible.

Mix Ingredients: In a bowl, combine the Greek yogurt, grated and drained cucumber, minced garlic, chopped mint, chopped dill, olive oil, and lemon juice. Mix well.

Season: Season the tzatziki with salt and pepper to taste. Adjust the seasoning according to your preference.

Chill: Cover the bowl and refrigerate the Minty Tzatziki for at least 30 minutes to allow the flavors to meld.

Serve: Give the tzatziki a final stir before serving. Garnish with additional mint leaves if desired.

Serve: Minty Tzatziki is a versatile sauce that goes well with grilled meats, falafel, pita bread, or as a refreshing dip for veggies. Enjoy this cool and herby yogurt sauce as a delightful addition to your Mediterranean-inspired dishes!

Thyme-infused Roast Chicken

Ingredients:

- 1 whole chicken (about 4-5 pounds)
- 2 tablespoons fresh thyme leaves
- 4 cloves garlic, minced
- 2 tablespoons olive oil
- 1 lemon, sliced
- Salt and pepper, to taste
- 1 cup chicken broth (for basting and moisture)

Instructions:

Preheat Oven: Preheat your oven to 375°F (190°C).

Prepare Chicken: Rinse the whole chicken under cold water and pat it dry with paper towels. Season the chicken cavity with salt and pepper.

Thyme Rub: In a small bowl, mix together the fresh thyme leaves, minced garlic, olive oil, salt, and pepper. Rub this thyme mixture all over the surface of the chicken, ensuring it's evenly coated.

Lemon Slices: Place the lemon slices under the skin of the chicken and inside the cavity for added flavor.

Truss Chicken (Optional): If you prefer, truss the chicken using kitchen twine to keep its shape and ensure even cooking.

Roasting: Place the seasoned and trussed chicken in a roasting pan. Pour the chicken broth into the bottom of the pan for basting and to keep the chicken moist during cooking.

Roast Chicken: Roast the chicken in the preheated oven for approximately 1.5 to 2 hours, or until the internal temperature reaches 165°F (74°C) in the thickest part of the thigh. Baste the chicken with pan juices every 30 minutes.

Resting: Once the chicken is cooked, remove it from the oven and let it rest for about 15 minutes before carving.

Serve: Carve the thyme-infused roast chicken and serve it with your favorite side dishes.

This thyme-infused roast chicken is not only flavorful but also aromatic. It's perfect for a family dinner or special occasions. Enjoy!

Dill Pickle Potato Salad

Ingredients:

- 2 pounds red potatoes, boiled and cubed
- 1 cup mayonnaise
- 1/4 cup Dijon mustard
- 1/4 cup dill pickles, finely chopped
- 2 tablespoons dill pickle juice
- 1/4 cup red onion, finely chopped
- 2 tablespoons fresh dill, chopped
- Salt and pepper, to taste
- 4 hard-boiled eggs, chopped (optional for garnish)

Instructions:

Prepare Potatoes: Boil the red potatoes until they are fork-tender. Allow them to cool, then cube them into bite-sized pieces.

Make Dressing: In a large bowl, whisk together the mayonnaise, Dijon mustard, dill pickle juice, salt, and pepper. Adjust the seasoning to taste.

Combine Ingredients: Add the cubed potatoes, chopped dill pickles, red onion, and fresh dill to the dressing. Gently toss everything together until the potatoes are well coated.

Chill: Cover the bowl and refrigerate the Dill Pickle Potato Salad for at least 2 hours to allow the flavors to meld.

Optional Garnish: Just before serving, garnish the potato salad with chopped hard-boiled eggs if desired.

Serve: Serve the Dill Pickle Potato Salad as a refreshing side dish at barbecues, picnics, or alongside grilled meats.

This potato salad combines the tangy crunch of dill pickles with creamy potatoes for a delightful twist on the classic. Enjoy!

Lemon-Herb Grilled Fish

Ingredients:

- 4 fish fillets (such as tilapia, salmon, or cod)
- 3 tablespoons olive oil
- 2 tablespoons fresh lemon juice
- 2 cloves garlic, minced
- 1 teaspoon lemon zest
- 1 teaspoon dried oregano
- 1 teaspoon dried thyme
- Salt and pepper, to taste
- Lemon wedges, for serving

Instructions:

Prepare Marinade: In a bowl, whisk together olive oil, lemon juice, minced garlic, lemon zest, dried oregano, dried thyme, salt, and pepper to create the marinade.

Marinate Fish: Place the fish fillets in a shallow dish or a resealable plastic bag. Pour the marinade over the fish, ensuring each fillet is well-coated. Marinate in the refrigerator for at least 30 minutes, allowing the flavors to infuse.

Preheat Grill: Preheat the grill to medium-high heat.

Grill Fish: Remove the fish from the marinade and discard the excess liquid. Grill the fish fillets for about 3-4 minutes per side, or until they are cooked through and easily flake with a fork.

Serve: Transfer the grilled fish to a serving platter. Squeeze fresh lemon wedges over the top for an extra burst of citrus flavor.

Garnish (Optional): Garnish with additional fresh herbs, such as chopped parsley, for a vibrant finish.

Serve: Serve the Lemon-Herb Grilled Fish with your favorite sides, such as steamed vegetables, rice, or a crisp salad.

This recipe creates a light and zesty dish perfect for summer grilling. Enjoy the delightful combination of lemon and herbs with your favorite fish!

Chimichurri Sauce

Ingredients:

- 1 cup fresh parsley, finely chopped
- 1/4 cup fresh cilantro, finely chopped
- 4 cloves garlic, minced
- 1/2 cup extra-virgin olive oil
- 2 tablespoons red wine vinegar
- 1 tablespoon fresh oregano, chopped
- 1 teaspoon red pepper flakes (adjust to taste)
- Salt and pepper, to taste

Instructions:

Prepare Herbs: Finely chop the fresh parsley, cilantro, and oregano.
Combine Ingredients: In a bowl, combine the chopped parsley, cilantro, minced garlic, chopped oregano, red pepper flakes, and a pinch of salt and pepper.
Add Liquid Ingredients: Pour in the extra-virgin olive oil and red wine vinegar.
Mix Well: Stir the ingredients together until well combined. Taste and adjust the seasoning if needed.
Resting Time: Allow the chimichurri sauce to rest for at least 15-20 minutes before serving to let the flavors meld.
Serve: Use Chimichurri Sauce as a condiment for grilled meats, such as steak or chicken. It can also be drizzled over roasted vegetables or used as a marinade.
Storage: Store any leftover chimichurri sauce in a sealed container in the refrigerator for up to a week.

Chimichurri adds a burst of freshness and tang to your dishes, making it a versatile and delicious accompaniment. Enjoy!

Mint Chocolate Chip Ice Cream

Ingredients:

- 2 cups heavy cream
- 1 cup whole milk
- 3/4 cup granulated sugar
- 1 teaspoon pure peppermint extract
- 1 teaspoon pure vanilla extract
- Green food coloring (optional, for color)
- 1 cup chocolate chips or chopped chocolate

Instructions:

Mix Base: In a mixing bowl, whisk together the heavy cream, whole milk, granulated sugar, peppermint extract, and vanilla extract until the sugar is fully dissolved.
Coloring (Optional): If desired, add a few drops of green food coloring to achieve the desired mint color. Mix well.
Chill Mixture: Cover the bowl and refrigerate the mixture for at least 2-4 hours or overnight. This allows the flavors to meld and the mixture to chill thoroughly.
Freeze: Pour the chilled mixture into an ice cream maker and churn according to the manufacturer's instructions.
Add Chocolate: In the last few minutes of churning, add the chocolate chips or chopped chocolate to evenly distribute throughout the ice cream.
Transfer and Freeze: Transfer the churned ice cream to a lidded container. Smooth the top, cover, and freeze for at least 4-6 hours or until firm.
Serve: Once fully frozen, scoop the Mint Chocolate Chip Ice Cream into bowls or cones. Enjoy!

This homemade mint chocolate chip ice cream is refreshing and loaded with chocolatey goodness. Adjust the mint flavor and sweetness according to your taste preferences. Enjoy!

Herb-Marinated Grilled Lamb Chops

Ingredients:

- 8 lamb chops
- 1/4 cup olive oil
- 3 tablespoons fresh rosemary, chopped
- 3 tablespoons fresh thyme, chopped
- 4 cloves garlic, minced
- Zest of 1 lemon
- Juice of 1 lemon
- Salt and black pepper, to taste

Instructions:

Prepare Marinade: In a bowl, combine the olive oil, chopped rosemary, chopped thyme, minced garlic, lemon zest, and lemon juice. Mix well.

Marinate Lamb Chops: Place the lamb chops in a shallow dish or a resealable plastic bag. Pour the marinade over the lamb chops, ensuring each chop is well-coated. Massage the marinade into the meat. Cover and refrigerate for at least 2 hours, or preferably overnight, to allow the flavors to infuse.

Preheat Grill: Preheat your grill to medium-high heat.

Grill Lamb Chops: Remove the lamb chops from the marinade and let any excess drip off. Season with salt and black pepper. Grill the lamb chops for about 3-4 minutes per side, or until they reach your desired doneness.

Resting Time: Allow the grilled lamb chops to rest for a few minutes before serving to let the juices redistribute.

Serve: Arrange the lamb chops on a serving platter. Garnish with additional fresh herbs if desired. Serve hot and enjoy!

These herb-marinated grilled lamb chops are flavorful and make a fantastic main course for a special meal. Pair them with your favorite side dishes for a complete and delicious experience.

Chive and Garlic Mashed Potatoes

Ingredients:

- 4 large potatoes, peeled and cut into chunks
- 4 cloves garlic, minced
- 1/2 cup butter
- 1/2 cup milk
- Salt and pepper, to taste
- 1/4 cup fresh chives, chopped

Instructions:

Boil Potatoes: Place the potato chunks in a large pot of salted water. Bring to a boil and cook until the potatoes are tender (about 15-20 minutes).

Prepare Garlic Butter: While the potatoes are cooking, melt the butter in a small pan over medium heat. Add the minced garlic and sauté for 1-2 minutes until fragrant. Remove from heat.

Drain and Mash: Drain the cooked potatoes and return them to the pot. Mash the potatoes using a potato masher or a fork.

Add Garlic Butter: Pour the garlic butter over the mashed potatoes and mix well.

Add Milk: Gradually add the milk while continuing to mash until the potatoes reach your desired consistency.

Season: Season the mashed potatoes with salt and pepper to taste. Adjust the seasoning as needed.

Stir in Chives: Fold in the chopped fresh chives, reserving some for garnish.

Serve: Transfer the chive and garlic mashed potatoes to a serving dish. Garnish with additional chives.

These flavorful mashed potatoes with chives and garlic make a perfect side dish for various meals. Enjoy!

Spice Recipes:

Homemade Garam Masala

Ingredients:

- 2 tablespoons cumin seeds
- 2 tablespoons coriander seeds
- 1 tablespoon cardamom pods
- 1 tablespoon black peppercorns
- 1 teaspoon whole cloves
- 1 teaspoon fennel seeds
- 1 cinnamon stick (about 3 inches)
- 1 dried bay leaf
- 1 teaspoon ground nutmeg (optional)

Instructions:

> Toast Whole Spices: In a dry skillet over medium heat, toast the cumin seeds, coriander seeds, cardamom pods, black peppercorns, cloves, and fennel seeds. Stir frequently and toast until fragrant, but be careful not to burn them. This usually takes about 2-3 minutes.
> Grind: Allow the toasted spices to cool slightly, then transfer them to a spice grinder or mortar and pestle. Grind the spices into a fine powder.
> Add Cinnamon and Bay Leaf: Add the ground spice mixture to a bowl. Grind the cinnamon stick and bay leaf separately, then add them to the bowl.
> Optional Nutmeg: If using nutmeg, either add it to the spice grinder with the other spices or grate it separately and add it to the bowl.
> Mix Well: Mix all the ground spices thoroughly until well combined.
> Store: Transfer the homemade garam masala to an airtight container. Store it in a cool, dark place.
> Use in Recipes: Use your homemade garam masala in various Indian dishes, curries, stews, and marinades for an authentic and aromatic flavor.

Feel free to adjust the quantities of individual spices to suit your taste preferences.

Homemade garam masala adds a rich and warming flavor to your dishes. Enjoy!

Chili Powder

Ingredients:

- 2 tablespoons ground cumin
- 2 tablespoons ground paprika
- 2 tablespoons ground coriander
- 1 tablespoon garlic powder
- 1 tablespoon onion powder
- 1 teaspoon cayenne pepper (adjust to taste for spice level)
- 1 teaspoon oregano
- 1 teaspoon thyme
- 1 teaspoon ground black pepper
- 1 teaspoon salt

Instructions:

Measure Spices: Gather all the ground spices - cumin, paprika, coriander, garlic powder, onion powder, cayenne pepper, oregano, thyme, black pepper, and salt.
Mix Well: In a bowl, combine all the measured spices. Mix well until the spices are evenly distributed.
Adjust Spice Level: Taste the chili powder and adjust the cayenne pepper to achieve your desired level of spiciness.
Store: Transfer the homemade chili powder to an airtight container. Store it in a cool, dark place.
Use in Recipes: Use your homemade chili powder in chili recipes, spice rubs, marinades, or any dish that calls for a warm and flavorful kick.

Making your own chili powder allows you to customize the flavor and heat level to suit your preferences. Enjoy experimenting with this spice blend in your favorite recipes!

Five-Spice Powder

Ingredients:

- 1 tablespoon ground cinnamon
- 1 tablespoon ground cloves
- 1 tablespoon fennel seeds, toasted and ground
- 1 tablespoon Sichuan peppercorns, toasted and ground
- 1 tablespoon star anise, ground

Instructions:

Prepare Spices: Toast the fennel seeds and Sichuan peppercorns in a dry skillet over medium heat until fragrant. Allow them to cool before grinding.
Grind Spices: Grind the toasted fennel seeds and Sichuan peppercorns using a spice grinder or mortar and pestle.
Combine Ingredients: In a bowl, combine the ground cinnamon, ground cloves, ground fennel seeds, ground Sichuan peppercorns, and ground star anise.
Mix Well: Mix the spices thoroughly until well combined. Ensure an even distribution of flavors.
Store: Transfer the homemade Five-Spice Powder to an airtight container. Store it in a cool, dark place.
Use in Recipes: Use your homemade Five-Spice Powder in various Chinese and Asian dishes, marinades, and sauces to add a distinctive and aromatic flavor.

Feel free to adjust the quantities to suit your taste preferences. Homemade Five-Spice Powder brings a complex and delightful flavor to your culinary creations. Enjoy!

Smoky Paprika Chicken

Ingredients:

- 4 boneless, skinless chicken breasts
- 2 teaspoons smoked paprika
- 1 teaspoon sweet paprika
- 1 teaspoon garlic powder
- 1 teaspoon onion powder
- 1/2 teaspoon dried oregano
- 1/2 teaspoon ground cumin
- Salt and black pepper, to taste
- 2 tablespoons olive oil
- Fresh parsley, chopped (for garnish)

Instructions:

Preheat Oven: Preheat your oven to 375°F (190°C).
Season Chicken: In a small bowl, mix together the smoked paprika, sweet paprika, garlic powder, onion powder, dried oregano, ground cumin, salt, and black pepper.
Coat Chicken: Rub the spice mixture evenly over both sides of each chicken breast, ensuring they are well coated.
Sear Chicken: Heat olive oil in an oven-safe skillet over medium-high heat. Sear the chicken breasts for 2-3 minutes on each side until they develop a golden brown crust.
Bake: Transfer the skillet to the preheated oven and bake for 20-25 minutes or until the chicken is cooked through and reaches an internal temperature of 165°F (74°C).
Rest and Serve: Remove the chicken from the oven and let it rest for a few minutes. Garnish with fresh chopped parsley before serving.
Serve: Slice the chicken and serve it with your favorite side dishes, such as roasted vegetables, rice, or a salad.

This Smoky Paprika Chicken is packed with flavor and has a delightful smokiness from the paprika. Enjoy your delicious and easy-to-make meal!

Curry Powder

Ingredients:

- 2 tablespoons ground coriander
- 2 tablespoons ground cumin
- 1 tablespoon ground turmeric
- 1 tablespoon ground ginger
- 1 teaspoon ground cinnamon
- 1 teaspoon ground cardamom
- 1 teaspoon ground cloves
- 1 teaspoon ground black pepper
- 1/2 teaspoon cayenne pepper (adjust to taste for spice level)

Instructions:

Gather Spices: Measure out the ground coriander, ground cumin, ground turmeric, ground ginger, ground cinnamon, ground cardamom, ground cloves, ground black pepper, and cayenne pepper.
Mix Spices: In a bowl, combine all the measured spices. Mix well until the spices are evenly distributed.
Adjust Spice Level: Taste the curry powder and adjust the cayenne pepper to achieve your desired level of spiciness.
Store: Transfer the homemade curry powder to an airtight container. Store it in a cool, dark place.
Use in Recipes: Use your homemade curry powder in a variety of curry dishes, stews, soups, and marinades for a burst of rich and aromatic flavor.

Feel free to experiment with the proportions and types of spices to tailor the curry powder to your liking. Enjoy creating delicious curries with your homemade spice blend!

Za'atar Roasted Vegetables

Ingredients:

- 4 cups mixed vegetables, such as cherry tomatoes, zucchini, bell peppers, and red onions, chopped into bite-sized pieces
- 2 tablespoons olive oil
- 2 tablespoons za'atar spice blend
- 1 teaspoon ground cumin
- 1 teaspoon ground coriander
- Salt and black pepper, to taste
- Fresh parsley, chopped (for garnish)

Instructions:

Preheat Oven: Preheat your oven to 400°F (200°C).
Prepare Vegetables: In a large mixing bowl, toss the mixed vegetables with olive oil, za'atar spice blend, ground cumin, ground coriander, salt, and black pepper. Ensure the vegetables are well coated with the seasoning.
Spread on Baking Sheet: Spread the seasoned vegetables in a single layer on a baking sheet lined with parchment paper.
Roast: Roast the vegetables in the preheated oven for 20-25 minutes or until they are tender and have developed a nice golden brown color, stirring once halfway through.
Garnish: Remove the roasted vegetables from the oven. Sprinkle with fresh chopped parsley for added freshness and flavor.
Serve: Transfer the Za'atar Roasted Vegetables to a serving dish and serve them as a delicious and aromatic side dish.

Feel free to customize the vegetable mix based on your preferences. This recipe brings out the unique flavors of za'atar while enhancing the natural goodness of roasted vegetables. Enjoy your flavorful and nutritious dish!

Cajun Shrimp Pasta

Ingredients:

- 8 oz (about 225g) linguine or fettuccine pasta
- 1 pound (about 450g) large shrimp, peeled and deveined
- 2 tablespoons Cajun seasoning
- 3 tablespoons olive oil
- 4 cloves garlic, minced
- 1 cup cherry tomatoes, halved
- 1 cup heavy cream
- 1/2 cup chicken broth
- 1/2 cup grated Parmesan cheese
- Salt and black pepper, to taste
- Fresh parsley, chopped (for garnish)
- Lemon wedges (optional)

Instructions:

Cook Pasta: Cook the pasta according to the package instructions until al dente. Drain and set aside.

Season Shrimp: In a bowl, toss the shrimp with Cajun seasoning, ensuring they are evenly coated.

Sear Shrimp: Heat 2 tablespoons of olive oil in a large skillet over medium-high heat. Add the seasoned shrimp and cook for 2-3 minutes per side until they are pink and opaque. Remove the shrimp from the skillet and set aside.

Saute Garlic and Tomatoes: In the same skillet, add the remaining 1 tablespoon of olive oil. Add minced garlic and halved cherry tomatoes. Sauté for 2-3 minutes until the tomatoes start to soften.

Make Sauce: Pour in the heavy cream and chicken broth. Bring the mixture to a simmer. Stir in the grated Parmesan cheese and let it melt into the sauce. Season with salt and black pepper to taste.

Combine Ingredients: Add the cooked pasta and seared shrimp to the skillet. Toss everything together until the pasta and shrimp are coated with the creamy Cajun sauce.

Garnish and Serve: Garnish with chopped fresh parsley. Serve the Cajun Shrimp Pasta hot, and optionally, with lemon wedges on the side for a burst of citrus flavor.

Enjoy your flavorful and spicy Cajun Shrimp Pasta!

Japanese Shichimi Togarashi Spice Mix

Ingredients:

- 1 tablespoon ground red chili pepper (adjust to taste)
- 1 tablespoon ground sichuan pepper
- 1 tablespoon roasted sesame seeds
- 1 tablespoon dried orange peel
- 1 teaspoon ground ginger
- 1 teaspoon dried seaweed (nori), finely chopped
- 1 teaspoon poppy seeds
- 1/2 teaspoon ground black pepper

Instructions:

Prepare Ingredients: If your sesame seeds are not roasted, lightly toast them in a dry pan over medium heat until they become fragrant. Allow them to cool.
Grind Ingredients: In a spice grinder or mortar and pestle, grind the sichuan pepper, dried orange peel, and poppy seeds to a coarse texture. You want to maintain some texture for a more authentic feel.
Combine Ingredients: In a bowl, combine the ground sichuan pepper, dried orange peel, poppy seeds with the ground red chili pepper, ground ginger, chopped nori, roasted sesame seeds, and ground black pepper.
Mix Well: Mix all the ingredients well to ensure an even distribution of flavors.
Store: Transfer the Shichimi Togarashi Spice Mix to an airtight container and store it in a cool, dry place.

Usage:

Sprinkle Shichimi Togarashi over noodles, rice dishes, soups, grilled meats, or any dish you'd like to add a kick of umami and heat. Adjust the quantity based on your spice preference.

Enjoy the complex and vibrant flavors of this Japanese spice blend!

Turmeric Golden Milk

Ingredients:

- 1 cup unsweetened almond milk (or any milk of your choice)
- 1/2 teaspoon ground turmeric
- 1/4 teaspoon ground cinnamon
- 1/8 teaspoon ground ginger
- 1 tablespoon honey or maple syrup (adjust to taste)
- 1/2 teaspoon coconut oil (optional)
- A pinch of black pepper (enhances turmeric absorption)

Instructions:

Heat Milk: In a small saucepan, heat the almond milk over medium heat until it is warm but not boiling.
Mix Spices: In a separate bowl, mix the ground turmeric, cinnamon, and ginger to create a spice blend.
Whisk Spices Into Milk: Add the spice blend to the warm milk, whisking continuously to ensure the spices are well incorporated.
Add Sweetener: Stir in the honey or maple syrup to sweeten the golden milk. Adjust the sweetness according to your taste.
Optional: Add Coconut Oil and Pepper: For added creaminess, you can add coconut oil to the golden milk. Also, add a pinch of black pepper, as it enhances the absorption of curcumin, the active compound in turmeric.
Strain (Optional): If you prefer a smoother texture, you can strain the golden milk using a fine mesh sieve to remove any remaining spice particles.
Serve: Pour the Turmeric Golden Milk into a cup and enjoy it warm.

This soothing and aromatic beverage is not only delicious but is also known for its potential health benefits, thanks to the anti-inflammatory properties of turmeric. Feel free to adjust the spice levels and sweetness to suit your preferences.

Blackened Cajun Salmon

Ingredients:

- 4 salmon fillets
- 2 tablespoons Cajun seasoning
- 1 teaspoon paprika
- 1 teaspoon onion powder
- 1 teaspoon garlic powder
- 1/2 teaspoon dried thyme
- 1/2 teaspoon dried oregano
- 1/2 teaspoon cayenne pepper (adjust to taste)
- Salt and black pepper to taste
- 2 tablespoons olive oil
- Lemon wedges for serving

Instructions:

Preheat the Oven: Preheat your oven to 400°F (200°C).
Prepare Cajun Spice Mix: In a small bowl, mix together the Cajun seasoning, paprika, onion powder, garlic powder, dried thyme, dried oregano, cayenne pepper, salt, and black pepper.
Season Salmon: Pat the salmon fillets dry with paper towels. Rub the Cajun spice mix generously over both sides of each salmon fillet.
Heat Olive Oil: In an oven-safe skillet, heat olive oil over medium-high heat.
Sear Salmon: Once the oil is hot, carefully place the salmon fillets in the skillet, skin side down. Sear for 2-3 minutes until the skin becomes crispy.
Transfer to Oven: Transfer the skillet to the preheated oven. Bake for 8-10 minutes or until the salmon is cooked through and flakes easily with a fork.
Serve: Remove the skillet from the oven. Serve the blackened Cajun salmon hot, garnished with lemon wedges.

Enjoy the bold and spicy flavors of this Blackened Cajun Salmon. Serve it alongside your favorite sides like rice, quinoa, or a fresh salad for a complete and delicious meal.

Adjust the level of cayenne pepper according to your spice preference.

Chinese Five-Spice Roasted Nuts

Ingredients:

- 2 cups mixed nuts (almonds, walnuts, cashews, pecans, etc.)
- 1 tablespoon vegetable oil
- 1 tablespoon Chinese five-spice powder
- 2 tablespoons honey
- 1/2 teaspoon salt (adjust to taste)
- 1/4 teaspoon cayenne pepper (optional, for added heat)

Instructions:

Preheat Oven: Preheat your oven to 325°F (163°C). Line a baking sheet with parchment paper.

Mix Nuts and Oil: In a bowl, combine the mixed nuts and vegetable oil. Toss the nuts until they are evenly coated with the oil.

Add Five-Spice Powder: Sprinkle the Chinese five-spice powder over the nuts. Toss again to ensure that the spice powder coats the nuts evenly.

Drizzle Honey: Drizzle the honey over the spiced nuts. Toss once more to coat the nuts with the honey.

Season with Salt and Cayenne (Optional): Sprinkle salt and cayenne pepper (if using) over the nuts and toss to combine. Adjust the salt and cayenne according to your taste preferences.

Spread on Baking Sheet: Spread the seasoned nuts in a single layer on the prepared baking sheet.

Roast in the Oven: Roast the nuts in the preheated oven for 15-20 minutes, stirring halfway through the baking time. Keep an eye on them to prevent burning.

Cool and Serve: Once the nuts are golden brown and fragrant, remove them from the oven and let them cool completely on the baking sheet.

Store: Once cooled, store the Chinese Five-Spice Roasted Nuts in an airtight container.

Enjoy these crunchy and spiced nuts as a snack or appetizer. The combination of Chinese five-spice powder and honey adds a unique and delicious flavor profile to the nuts. Adjust the spice levels and sweetness to suit your taste preferences.

Condiments Recipes:

Homemade Ketchup

Ingredients:

- 1 can (28 ounces) crushed tomatoes
- 1/2 cup apple cider vinegar
- 1/4 cup brown sugar (adjust to taste)
- 1 teaspoon onion powder
- 1 teaspoon garlic powder
- 1 teaspoon salt
- 1/2 teaspoon ground mustard
- 1/4 teaspoon allspice
- 1/4 teaspoon cinnamon
- 1/4 teaspoon cloves
- 1/4 teaspoon black pepper

Instructions:

> Combine Ingredients: In a medium saucepan, combine the crushed tomatoes, apple cider vinegar, brown sugar, onion powder, garlic powder, salt, ground mustard, allspice, cinnamon, cloves, and black pepper.
> Simmer: Bring the mixture to a simmer over medium heat. Stir well to combine all the ingredients.
> Cook: Reduce the heat to low and let the mixture simmer gently for about 45-60 minutes, stirring occasionally. The ketchup should thicken and develop a rich flavor.
> Adjust Consistency: If the ketchup is too thick for your liking, you can add a bit of water to reach your desired consistency.
> Taste and Adjust: Taste the ketchup and adjust the seasoning, adding more sugar or salt if needed.
> Blend (Optional): For a smoother texture, you can use an immersion blender or transfer the mixture to a blender to puree until smooth.
> Cool and Store: Allow the homemade ketchup to cool completely. Once cooled, transfer it to a clean glass jar or container and refrigerate.
> Serve: Use your homemade ketchup as a condiment for burgers, fries, or any dish where ketchup is enjoyed.

Enjoy your flavorful and preservative-free Homemade Ketchup! Adjust the sweetness and spices to suit your taste preferences.

Garlic Aioli

Ingredients:

- 1 cup mayonnaise
- 3 cloves garlic, minced
- 1 tablespoon Dijon mustard
- 1 tablespoon fresh lemon juice
- Salt and pepper to taste
- 2 tablespoons fresh parsley, chopped (optional)

Instructions:

Mince Garlic: Peel and mince the garlic cloves finely.
Combine Ingredients: In a bowl, combine mayonnaise, minced garlic, Dijon mustard, and fresh lemon juice. Mix well to ensure the ingredients are thoroughly combined.
Season: Season the aioli with salt and pepper to taste. Adjust the seasoning according to your preferences.
Optional: Add Fresh Parsley: If desired, add chopped fresh parsley to the aioli for added flavor and freshness.
Mix Well: Stir the ingredients until well combined. Make sure the minced garlic is evenly distributed throughout the aioli.
Chill (Optional): For enhanced flavor, refrigerate the garlic aioli for at least 30 minutes before serving. This allows the flavors to meld.
Serve: Use the garlic aioli as a dipping sauce for fries, a spread for sandwiches, or a flavorful accompaniment for grilled meats, seafood, or vegetables.
Store: Store any leftover aioli in a sealed container in the refrigerator for up to a week.

This homemade Garlic Aioli adds a burst of garlic and tangy flavor to your favorite dishes. Feel free to customize the recipe by adjusting the garlic, lemon, or other seasonings to match your taste preferences.

Salsa Verde

Ingredients:

- 1 pound tomatillos, husked and rinsed
- 2-3 medium-sized jalapeño peppers (adjust to taste)
- 1/2 cup chopped onion
- 2 cloves garlic, minced
- 1/2 cup fresh cilantro, chopped
- 1 tablespoon lime juice
- Salt to taste

Instructions:

Prepare Tomatillos: Remove the husks from the tomatillos and rinse them under cold water to remove any sticky residue.
Roast Tomatillos and Peppers: Place the tomatillos and jalapeño peppers on a baking sheet. Broil in the oven or roast on a stovetop burner until they are slightly charred. Turn them to ensure even roasting.
Cool: Allow the roasted tomatillos and peppers to cool to room temperature.
Blend: In a blender or food processor, combine the roasted tomatillos, jalapeños, chopped onion, minced garlic, cilantro, and lime juice.
Blend Until Smooth: Pulse the ingredients until you achieve your desired consistency. Some people prefer a chunkier salsa, while others like it smoother.
Season: Add salt to taste and blend again to incorporate the salt evenly.
Adjust Heat: Taste the salsa and adjust the heat level by adding more jalapeño if desired. You can also remove the seeds and membranes for a milder version.
Chill (Optional): Refrigerate the salsa for at least 30 minutes before serving to allow the flavors to meld.
Serve: Salsa Verde is ready to be served! Enjoy it with tortilla chips, tacos, grilled meats, or as a condiment for various dishes.
Store: Store any leftover Salsa Verde in a sealed container in the refrigerator. It can be stored for several days.

Feel free to customize the recipe by adding ingredients like avocado or adjusting the levels of cilantro, garlic, or lime juice to suit your taste preferences.

Honey Mustard Sauce

Ingredients:

- 1/2 cup Dijon mustard
- 1/4 cup honey
- 2 tablespoons mayonnaise
- 1 tablespoon apple cider vinegar
- Salt and pepper to taste

Instructions:

Combine Ingredients: In a bowl, whisk together Dijon mustard, honey, mayonnaise, and apple cider vinegar until well combined.

Adjust Consistency: If you prefer a thinner consistency, you can add a bit more honey or vinegar. For a thicker sauce, adjust with additional mustard.

Season: Taste the sauce and season with salt and pepper according to your preferences. Keep in mind that the mustard may add some saltiness, so adjust accordingly.

Whisk Until Smooth: Whisk the ingredients together until the sauce is smooth and well incorporated.

Chill (Optional): For enhanced flavor, you can refrigerate the Honey Mustard Sauce for at least 30 minutes before serving. This allows the flavors to meld.

Serve: Use the Honey Mustard Sauce as a dipping sauce for chicken tenders, pretzels, or vegetables. It also makes a tasty dressing for salads or a glaze for grilled meats.

Store: Store any unused Honey Mustard Sauce in a sealed container in the refrigerator. It can be kept for several days.

Feel free to customize the recipe by adjusting the ratio of honey to mustard or adding additional ingredients like garlic, herbs, or spices to suit your taste preferences.

Harissa Paste

Ingredients:

- 6-8 dried red chili peppers (such as guajillo or ancho), seeds removed
- 3 cloves garlic, minced
- 1 teaspoon ground cumin
- 1 teaspoon ground coriander
- 1 teaspoon caraway seeds
- 1 teaspoon smoked paprika
- 1/2 teaspoon ground cinnamon
- 1/4 cup tomato paste
- 2 tablespoons olive oil
- 1 tablespoon lemon juice
- Salt to taste

Instructions:

Prepare Chili Peppers: If the dried chili peppers are not soft, soak them in hot water for about 30 minutes until they become pliable. Remove the seeds for a milder harissa or leave them in for extra heat.

Toast Spices: In a dry skillet over medium heat, toast the cumin, coriander, caraway seeds, and smoked paprika for 1-2 minutes until fragrant. Be careful not to burn them.

Blend Ingredients: In a blender or food processor, combine the soaked chili peppers, toasted spices, minced garlic, tomato paste, olive oil, lemon juice, and a pinch of salt.

Blend Until Smooth: Blend the ingredients until you achieve a smooth and thick paste. You may need to scrape down the sides of the blender or processor and blend again to ensure everything is well incorporated.

Adjust Consistency and Seasoning: If the harissa is too thick, you can add a bit more olive oil or water until you reach your desired consistency. Taste the harissa and adjust the salt and acidity (lemon juice) to suit your preferences.

Store: Transfer the harissa paste to a jar or airtight container. Drizzle a thin layer of olive oil on top to help preserve it. Store in the refrigerator for up to a few weeks.

Usage:

- Use harissa paste as a marinade for meats or vegetables.
- Mix it into couscous or rice for added flavor.
- Stir it into soups, stews, or sauces.
- Spread it on sandwiches or wraps for a spicy kick.

Feel free to customize the recipe by adjusting the spice levels or experimenting with additional ingredients like sun-dried tomatoes or fresh herbs.

Avocado Lime Crema

Ingredients:

- 1 ripe avocado, peeled and pitted
- 1/2 cup sour cream or Greek yogurt
- 1 clove garlic, minced
- Juice of 1-2 limes (adjust to taste)
- 2 tablespoons fresh cilantro, chopped
- Salt and pepper to taste

Instructions:

Prepare Avocado: In a bowl, mash the ripe avocado using a fork or spoon until smooth.

Combine Ingredients: Add the sour cream or Greek yogurt, minced garlic, lime juice, and chopped cilantro to the mashed avocado.

Mix Well: Mix all the ingredients together until well combined. You can use a fork or whisk to ensure a smooth and creamy consistency.

Season: Season the crema with salt and pepper according to your taste preferences. Stir well to incorporate the seasonings.

Adjust Consistency: If the crema is too thick, you can add a little water or more lime juice to achieve your desired consistency. Mix until smooth.

Taste and Adjust: Taste the Avocado Lime Crema and adjust the lime juice, salt, or other seasonings if needed. The lime should provide a zesty flavor to complement the creaminess of the avocado.

Chill (Optional): For best results, you can refrigerate the crema for at least 30 minutes before serving to allow the flavors to meld. This step is optional but enhances the taste.

Serve: Use Avocado Lime Crema as a topping for tacos, grilled chicken, fish, or as a dip for vegetables. It adds a delicious and creamy element to a variety of dishes.

Feel free to customize the recipe by adding ingredients like jalapeños for extra heat or adjusting the cilantro and lime quantities based on your preferences.

Homemade Sriracha Sauce

Ingredients:

- 1 pound red chili peppers (such as Fresno or red jalapeños), stems removed
- 4 cloves garlic, peeled
- 1 tablespoon brown sugar
- 1 teaspoon salt
- 1 cup distilled white vinegar
- 2 tablespoons fish sauce (or soy sauce for a vegetarian version)

Instructions:

Prepare Chilies: Roughly chop the red chili peppers, removing the stems. If you prefer a milder sauce, you can deseed the peppers.
Blend Ingredients: In a blender or food processor, combine the chopped chili peppers, peeled garlic cloves, brown sugar, and salt. Blend until you have a coarse paste.
Cook Mixture: Transfer the chili paste to a saucepan. Add the distilled white vinegar and fish sauce (or soy sauce). Bring the mixture to a simmer over medium heat.
Simmer: Reduce the heat to low and let the mixture simmer for about 15-20 minutes. Stir occasionally.
Blend Again (Optional): For a smoother sauce, you can blend the mixture again after it has simmered. Use caution when blending hot liquids; allow the mixture to cool slightly before blending.
Adjust Consistency: If the sauce is too thick, you can add a little water to reach your desired consistency.
Taste and Adjust: Taste the Sriracha sauce and adjust the seasoning if needed. You can add more sugar for sweetness or more salt for seasoning.
Cool and Store: Allow the Sriracha sauce to cool completely before transferring it to a clean, airtight jar or bottle. Store it in the refrigerator.
Maturation (Optional): The flavors of Sriracha tend to improve with time. If possible, let the sauce mature in the refrigerator for a few days before using.
Enjoy: Use your homemade Sriracha sauce as a condiment for various dishes, such as stir-fries, noodles, or as a dipping sauce.

Remember, you can adjust the recipe based on your heat tolerance and flavor preferences. Feel free to experiment with different types of chili peppers for a unique twist.

Cucumber Raita

Ingredients:

- 1 cup plain yogurt
- 1 cucumber, peeled and grated
- 1/2 teaspoon cumin powder
- 1/2 teaspoon coriander powder
- 1/4 teaspoon red chili powder (adjust to taste)
- 1 tablespoon fresh mint leaves, chopped
- 1 tablespoon fresh coriander leaves (cilantro), chopped
- Salt to taste
- 1/2 teaspoon roasted cumin seeds (optional, for garnish)
- Chopped fresh mint or coriander leaves for garnish

Instructions:

Prepare Cucumber: Peel the cucumber and grate it. You can also finely chop it if you prefer a chunkier texture.

Drain Excess Water: If the cucumber has a lot of water content, you can place it in a sieve or colander, sprinkle a little salt, and let it sit for about 10 minutes. Squeeze out any excess water.

Prepare Yogurt Base: In a mixing bowl, whisk the plain yogurt until smooth.

Add Cucumber and Spices: Add the grated cucumber to the yogurt. Add cumin powder, coriander powder, red chili powder, chopped mint leaves, chopped coriander leaves, and salt.

Mix Well: Mix all the ingredients well until they are evenly combined.

Adjust Seasoning: Taste the raita and adjust the seasoning according to your preference. You can add more salt or spice if needed.

Chill: Refrigerate the cucumber raita for at least 30 minutes before serving to allow the flavors to meld.

Garnish: Just before serving, garnish the raita with roasted cumin seeds and chopped fresh mint or coriander leaves.

Serve: Cucumber raita can be served as a side dish with various Indian dishes like biryani, curry, or kebabs. It also works well as a cooling accompaniment to spicy meals.

Enjoy your homemade cucumber raita!

Mango Salsa

Ingredients:

- 2 ripe mangoes, peeled, pitted, and diced
- 1/2 red onion, finely chopped
- 1 red bell pepper, diced
- 1 jalapeño, seeds removed and finely chopped (adjust to taste)
- 1/4 cup fresh cilantro, chopped
- Juice of 2 limes
- Salt and pepper to taste

Optional Additions:

- 1/2 cucumber, diced
- 1 avocado, diced
- 1 small tomato, diced

Instructions:

Prepare Ingredients: Peel, pit, and dice the ripe mangoes. Finely chop the red onion, red bell pepper, jalapeño, and cilantro.

Combine Ingredients: In a mixing bowl, combine the diced mangoes, red onion, red bell pepper, jalapeño, and cilantro. If you're adding optional ingredients like cucumber, avocado, or tomato, include them as well.

Add Lime Juice: Squeeze the juice of two limes over the mango mixture.

Season: Season the salsa with salt and pepper to taste. Stir well to combine.

Chill: Allow the mango salsa to chill in the refrigerator for at least 30 minutes to allow the flavors to meld.

Adjust Flavor: Taste the salsa and adjust the lime juice, salt, or pepper if needed.

Serve: Mango salsa is a versatile condiment that pairs well with grilled chicken, fish tacos, shrimp, or as a topping for salads. It can also be enjoyed with tortilla chips as a refreshing snack.

Feel free to customize the salsa according to your preferences, and enjoy the sweet and tangy flavors of this homemade mango salsa!

Chutney

Ingredients:

- 1 cup fresh mint leaves, washed and stems removed
- 1/2 cup fresh cilantro (coriander), washed
- 1 green chili, chopped (adjust to taste)
- 1 small onion, chopped
- 1 tablespoon fresh ginger, grated
- 2 tablespoons lemon juice
- 1 teaspoon cumin seeds
- 1/2 teaspoon salt (adjust to taste)
- 1/2 teaspoon sugar
- Water (as needed)

Optional Additions:

- 1/2 cup grated coconut
- 1 clove garlic
- Yogurt for a creamier texture

Instructions:

Prepare Ingredients: Wash the mint leaves and cilantro thoroughly. Remove the stems from the mint and chop the onion, green chili, and ginger.
Blend Ingredients: In a blender or food processor, combine the mint leaves, cilantro, chopped onion, green chili, grated ginger, lemon juice, cumin seeds, salt, and sugar. If you're adding optional ingredients like coconut or garlic, include them as well.
Blend Until Smooth: Blend the ingredients until you achieve a smooth consistency. If the mixture is too thick, you can add water in small increments to reach the desired consistency.
Adjust Seasoning: Taste the chutney and adjust the salt, sugar, or lemon juice according to your preference.
Chill: Allow the chutney to chill in the refrigerator for at least 30 minutes to enhance the flavors.
Serve: Mint chutney can be served as a condiment with various dishes such as samosas, pakoras, dosas, or as a side for grilled meats. It's also a great accompaniment to Indian snacks and appetizers.

Feel free to experiment with the ingredients and proportions to create a chutney that suits your taste. Enjoy the vibrant and tangy flavors of homemade mint chutney!

Balsamic Glaze

Ingredients:

- 1 cup balsamic vinegar
- 2 tablespoons honey or maple syrup (optional, for sweetness)

Instructions:

Combine Ingredients: In a small saucepan, combine the balsamic vinegar and honey or maple syrup (if using). Stir well to mix.
Heat Over Medium Heat: Place the saucepan over medium heat and bring the mixture to a gentle boil.
Reduce Heat and Simmer: Once it starts boiling, reduce the heat to low and let the mixture simmer. Allow it to simmer for about 15-20 minutes, or until the balsamic vinegar has thickened and reduced by half. Stir occasionally.
Check Consistency: To test the consistency, dip a spoon into the glaze. If it coats the back of the spoon and has a syrupy consistency, it's ready. Keep in mind that it will thicken further as it cools.
Cool and Store: Remove the saucepan from heat and let the balsamic glaze cool to room temperature. It will continue to thicken as it cools. Once cooled, transfer it to a glass jar or bottle for storage.
Serve: Drizzle the balsamic glaze over salads, roasted vegetables, grilled meats, or even desserts like strawberries and vanilla ice cream.

Feel free to adjust the sweetness to your liking by adding more or less honey or maple syrup. This homemade balsamic glaze adds a delightful touch to a variety of dishes, enhancing both the flavor and presentation.

Specialty Herb and Spice Blends:

Herbes de Provence

Ingredients:

- 2 tablespoons dried thyme
- 2 tablespoons dried rosemary
- 2 tablespoons dried marjoram
- 2 tablespoons dried oregano
- 1 tablespoon dried savory
- 1 tablespoon dried lavender flowers (optional)

Instructions:

Mix Herbs: In a bowl, combine all the dried herbs. If using lavender flowers, make sure they are food-grade and not treated with any chemicals.

Crush or Grind (Optional): For a more integrated flavor, you can use a mortar and pestle or a spice grinder to crush or grind the herbs slightly. This step is optional and depends on personal preference.

Store: Transfer the Herbes de Provence mixture to an airtight container, such as a glass jar, and store it in a cool, dark place.

Use: Sprinkle the Herbes de Provence blend onto roasted vegetables, grilled meats, poultry, or in soups and stews to add a touch of the Mediterranean to your dishes.

Feel free to adjust the ratios of herbs according to your taste preferences. This versatile herb blend can be a delightful addition to various recipes, bringing a taste of the French countryside to your kitchen.

Ras el Hanout

Ingredients:

- 1 teaspoon ground cumin
- 1 teaspoon ground ginger
- 1 teaspoon ground cinnamon
- 1 teaspoon ground coriander
- 1 teaspoon ground paprika
- 1 teaspoon ground turmeric
- 1/2 teaspoon ground cloves
- 1/2 teaspoon ground nutmeg
- 1/2 teaspoon ground allspice
- 1/2 teaspoon cayenne pepper (adjust to taste)
- 1/2 teaspoon ground cardamom
- 1/2 teaspoon ground black pepper
- 1/4 teaspoon ground fenugreek (optional)
- 1/4 teaspoon ground fennel seeds
- 1/4 teaspoon ground star anise

Instructions:

Combine Spices: In a bowl, mix together all the ground spices thoroughly.
Optional Toasting (Enhances Flavor): For an extra layer of flavor, you can toast whole spices like cumin seeds, coriander seeds, and black peppercorns in a dry pan until fragrant. Grind them before adding to the mix.
Store: Transfer the Ras el Hanout blend to an airtight container, such as a spice jar, and store it in a cool, dark place.
Use: Ras el Hanout can be used as a spice rub for meats, added to couscous, rice, tagines, stews, or used as a general seasoning to add complexity to various dishes.

Feel free to adjust the spice ratios according to your taste preferences. Ras el Hanout is known for its aromatic and warm flavor profile, making it a versatile spice blend in North African and Middle Eastern cuisines.

Italian Seasoning Blend

Ingredients:

- 1 tablespoon dried oregano
- 1 tablespoon dried basil
- 1 tablespoon dried thyme
- 1 tablespoon dried rosemary
- 1 tablespoon dried marjoram
- 1 tablespoon dried sage

Optional Additions:

- 1 teaspoon dried parsley
- 1 teaspoon garlic powder
- 1 teaspoon onion powder
- 1/2 teaspoon red pepper flakes (for a bit of heat)

Instructions:

Combine Herbs: In a bowl, mix together the dried oregano, basil, thyme, rosemary, marjoram, and sage.
Optional Additions: If you choose to add garlic powder, onion powder, dried parsley, or red pepper flakes for extra flavor, include them in the mix.
Blend Thoroughly: Mix all the ingredients thoroughly to ensure an even distribution of flavors.
Store: Transfer the Italian Seasoning blend to an airtight container, such as a spice jar, and store it in a cool, dark place.
Use: This Italian Seasoning blend is versatile and can be used in pasta sauces, marinades, dressings, on roasted vegetables, or as a seasoning for grilled meats.

Feel free to adjust the quantities to suit your taste preferences. Making your own Italian Seasoning allows you to customize the blend and enjoy the freshest flavors in your dishes.

Taco Seasoning Mix

Ingredients:

- 1 tablespoon chili powder
- 1 teaspoon ground cumin
- 1 teaspoon paprika
- 1 teaspoon garlic powder
- 1 teaspoon onion powder
- 1/2 teaspoon dried oregano
- 1/2 teaspoon smoked paprika (optional for added depth)
- 1/2 teaspoon red pepper flakes (adjust to taste for heat)
- 1/2 teaspoon ground coriander
- 1/2 teaspoon black pepper
- 1/2 teaspoon salt (adjust to taste)

Instructions:

Combine Ingredients: In a bowl, mix together chili powder, cumin, paprika, garlic powder, onion powder, dried oregano, smoked paprika (if using), red pepper flakes, ground coriander, black pepper, and salt.
Blend Thoroughly: Ensure all the spices are well blended for an even distribution of flavors.
Store: Transfer the Taco Seasoning Mix to an airtight container, such as a spice jar, and store it in a cool, dark place.
Use: This homemade Taco Seasoning Mix is perfect for seasoning ground beef, chicken, or beans for tacos, burritos, or other Mexican-inspired dishes. Adjust the quantity to your taste preferences.

By making your own taco seasoning, you can control the ingredients and customize the spice level to suit your preferences. Enjoy!

Adobe Seasoning

Ingredients:

- 1 tablespoon garlic powder
- 1 tablespoon onion powder
- 1 tablespoon dried oregano
- 1 tablespoon ground cumin
- 1 tablespoon paprika
- 1 teaspoon black pepper
- 1 teaspoon salt

Instructions:

In a bowl, combine garlic powder, onion powder, dried oregano, ground cumin, paprika, black pepper, and salt.
Mix thoroughly to ensure an even distribution of flavors.
Transfer the Adobo Seasoning to an airtight container and store it in a cool, dark place.
Use the Adobo Seasoning to add flavor to meats, poultry, fish, vegetables, or rice dishes. Adjust the quantity according to your taste preferences.

Feel free to customize the blend by adding other spices like coriander, turmeric, or chili powder based on your liking. Enjoy your homemade Adobo Seasoning!

Berbere Spice Blend

Ingredients:

- 2 tablespoons paprika
- 1 tablespoon ground cumin
- 1 tablespoon ground coriander
- 1 tablespoon ground cardamom
- 1 tablespoon ground fenugreek
- 1 tablespoon ground cinnamon
- 1 teaspoon ground cloves
- 1 teaspoon ground allspice
- 1 teaspoon ground nutmeg
- 1 teaspoon ground ginger
- 1 teaspoon cayenne pepper (adjust to taste for heat)
- 1 teaspoon turmeric
- 1/2 teaspoon black pepper
- 1/2 teaspoon ground fenugreek seeds (optional)
- 1/2 teaspoon ground mustard seeds (optional)

Instructions:

In a bowl, combine all the spices, adjusting the quantities to your taste preferences.
Mix well to ensure an even distribution of the spices.
Transfer the Berbere Spice Blend to an airtight container and store it in a cool, dark place.
Use the Berbere Spice Blend to add depth and heat to stews, soups, lentil dishes, or as a dry rub for meats. Adjust the quantity based on the desired level of spiciness.

Feel free to experiment with the spice ratios to create a blend that suits your taste.

Berbere adds a rich and complex flavor to dishes, making it a versatile and aromatic spice mix. Enjoy your culinary adventures with Berbere Spice Blend!

Shawarma Seasoning

Ingredients:

- 1 tablespoon ground cumin
- 1 tablespoon ground coriander
- 1 tablespoon ground paprika
- 1 tablespoon ground turmeric
- 1 tablespoon ground cinnamon
- 1 tablespoon ground allspice
- 1 teaspoon ground cloves
- 1 teaspoon ground cardamom
- 1 teaspoon garlic powder
- 1 teaspoon onion powder
- 1 teaspoon cayenne pepper (adjust to taste for heat)
- Salt and black pepper to taste

Instructions:

In a bowl, combine all the ground spices and seasonings.
Adjust the quantities to your taste preferences and desired level of spiciness.
Mix the ingredients thoroughly to ensure an even distribution.
Use the Shawarma Seasoning to marinate chicken, beef, lamb, or your preferred protein before grilling, roasting, or cooking. You can also use it as a dry rub for meats.
Store the Shawarma Seasoning in an airtight container in a cool, dark place.

Feel free to customize the blend by experimenting with additional spices like sumac, nutmeg, or ginger for a unique flavor profile. Enjoy the delicious taste of homemade Shawarma Seasoning in your dishes!

Sesame Ginger Dressing

Ingredients:

- 3 tablespoons soy sauce
- 2 tablespoons rice vinegar
- 1 tablespoon sesame oil
- 1 tablespoon fresh ginger, grated
- 1 tablespoon honey or maple syrup
- 1 clove garlic, minced
- 2 tablespoons neutral oil (such as vegetable or canola oil)
- 1 teaspoon sesame seeds (optional)
- Salt and pepper to taste

Instructions:

In a bowl, whisk together soy sauce, rice vinegar, sesame oil, grated ginger, honey or maple syrup, and minced garlic.

Slowly drizzle in the neutral oil while whisking continuously to emulsify the dressing.

Taste the dressing and adjust the sweetness or saltiness according to your preference.

If desired, stir in sesame seeds for added texture.

Store the Sesame Ginger Dressing in an airtight container in the refrigerator. It's recommended to let the flavors meld for at least 30 minutes before using.

Shake or whisk the dressing well before serving.

Use this Sesame Ginger Dressing on salads, as a marinade for proteins, or as a dipping sauce. Enjoy the vibrant and zesty flavors!

Jerk Seasoning

Ingredients:

- 2 tablespoons ground allspice
- 2 teaspoons dried thyme
- 2 teaspoons paprika
- 1 teaspoon cayenne pepper (adjust to taste for heat)
- 1 teaspoon onion powder
- 1 teaspoon garlic powder
- 1 teaspoon sugar
- 1 teaspoon salt
- 1/2 teaspoon black pepper
- 1/2 teaspoon dried crushed red pepper flakes
- 1/2 teaspoon ground cinnamon
- 1/2 teaspoon ground nutmeg
- 2 tablespoons soy sauce
- 2 tablespoons vegetable oil
- 2 tablespoons apple cider vinegar
- Juice of 1 lime

Instructions:

In a bowl, combine all the dry spices and herbs: ground allspice, dried thyme, paprika, cayenne pepper, onion powder, garlic powder, sugar, salt, black pepper, crushed red pepper flakes, ground cinnamon, and ground nutmeg.
In a separate bowl, mix together the wet ingredients: soy sauce, vegetable oil, apple cider vinegar, and lime juice.
Gradually add the wet ingredients to the dry spice mixture, stirring well to create a thick paste.
Adjust the seasoning to taste, adding more salt, sugar, or cayenne pepper if needed.
Use the Jerk Seasoning as a marinade for chicken, pork, fish, or tofu. Allow the meat to marinate for at least a few hours or overnight for the best flavor.
Grill, bake, or cook the marinated protein until fully cooked and enjoy the authentic Jamaican jerk flavors.

Feel free to customize the recipe by adding additional herbs or spices to suit your taste preferences. Jerk seasoning adds a deliciously spicy and aromatic kick to your dishes.

Greek Souvlaki Marinade

Ingredients:

- 1/4 cup olive oil
- 1/4 cup lemon juice
- 3 cloves garlic, minced
- 1 teaspoon dried oregano
- 1 teaspoon dried thyme
- 1 teaspoon dried rosemary
- 1 teaspoon paprika
- 1 teaspoon ground cumin
- Salt and black pepper to taste
- 1 to 1.5 pounds of your choice of meat (chicken, pork, or lamb), cut into bite-sized pieces

Instructions:

In a bowl, whisk together the olive oil, lemon juice, minced garlic, dried oregano, dried thyme, dried rosemary, paprika, ground cumin, salt, and black pepper. Mix well to ensure all ingredients are combined.
Place the bite-sized meat pieces in a large resealable plastic bag or shallow dish. Pour the marinade over the meat, making sure all pieces are evenly coated. Seal the bag or cover the dish and refrigerate for at least 1-2 hours, or preferably overnight for maximum flavor.
When ready to cook, preheat your grill or oven.
Thread the marinated meat onto skewers.
Grill the skewers over medium-high heat or bake in the oven until the meat is fully cooked and has a nice char on the outside.
Serve the Greek Souvlaki with pita bread, tzatziki sauce, and your favorite fresh vegetables.

This marinade infuses the meat with the quintessential Greek flavors, resulting in a delicious and aromatic dish. Adjust the seasoning to your taste and enjoy your homemade Greek Souvlaki!

Moroccan Ras el Hanout Hummus

Ingredients:

- 1 can (15 ounces) chickpeas, drained and rinsed
- 1/4 cup tahini
- 3 tablespoons olive oil
- 2 tablespoons lemon juice
- 2 cloves garlic, minced
- 1 teaspoon Moroccan Ras el Hanout spice blend
- 1/2 teaspoon ground cumin
- 1/2 teaspoon ground coriander
- 1/4 teaspoon smoked paprika
- Salt to taste
- 2-3 tablespoons water (as needed for desired consistency)
- Extra olive oil and sprinkle of Ras el Hanout for garnish

Instructions:

In a food processor, combine the chickpeas, tahini, olive oil, lemon juice, minced garlic, Ras el Hanout, cumin, coriander, smoked paprika, and a pinch of salt. Process the mixture until smooth, scraping down the sides as needed.
If the hummus is too thick, add water, one tablespoon at a time, until you reach your desired consistency.
Taste the hummus and adjust the seasoning, adding more salt or Ras el Hanout if needed.
Once the hummus is smooth and well-seasoned, transfer it to a serving bowl.
Drizzle the top with a bit of olive oil and sprinkle a pinch of Ras el Hanout for garnish.
Serve the Moroccan Ras el Hanout Hummus with pita bread, fresh vegetables, or as a flavorful spread.

This hummus is rich in Moroccan spices, offering a delightful and exotic flavor. Adjust the spice levels according to your preference, and enjoy the unique twist on a classic dip!

Homemade Sauces:

Hollandaise Sauce

Ingredients:

- 3 large egg yolks
- 1 tablespoon water
- 1 tablespoon lemon juice
- 1 cup (2 sticks) unsalted butter, melted
- Pinch of cayenne pepper
- Salt, to taste

Instructions:

In a heatproof bowl, whisk together the egg yolks, water, and lemon juice until well combined.
Place the bowl over a saucepan of simmering water, creating a double boiler. Make sure the bottom of the bowl does not touch the water.
Whisk the egg yolk mixture continuously until it begins to thicken. Be patient and avoid cooking too quickly; this process should take about 3-5 minutes.
Once the egg yolk mixture has thickened, slowly drizzle in the melted butter while whisking constantly. Continue whisking until the sauce becomes smooth and creamy.
If the sauce is too thick, you can add a little more water or lemon juice to reach your desired consistency.
Season the Hollandaise sauce with a pinch of cayenne pepper and salt to taste. Adjust the seasoning according to your preference.
Remove the sauce from heat and serve immediately.

Hollandaise Sauce is best served warm and pairs wonderfully with poached eggs, asparagus, or other vegetables. Keep in mind that this sauce is sensitive to heat, so it's recommended to serve it promptly after preparation. Enjoy this classic and indulgent sauce!

Soy-Ginger Glaze

Ingredients:

- 1/4 cup soy sauce
- 2 tablespoons rice vinegar
- 2 tablespoons honey
- 1 tablespoon fresh ginger, grated
- 2 cloves garlic, minced
- 1 teaspoon sesame oil
- 1 tablespoon cornstarch (optional, for thickening)

Instructions:

In a small bowl, whisk together soy sauce, rice vinegar, honey, grated ginger, minced garlic, and sesame oil.
If you prefer a thicker glaze, you can mix cornstarch with a tablespoon of water to create a slurry. Stir the slurry into the sauce mixture.
Transfer the sauce to a saucepan and heat over medium heat. Bring the mixture to a simmer, stirring continuously.
Let the glaze simmer for 2-3 minutes or until it thickens to your desired consistency. If you added cornstarch, make sure to cook it thoroughly to eliminate any starchy taste.
Once thickened, remove the glaze from heat and let it cool slightly.
Use the Soy-Ginger Glaze immediately to drizzle over grilled chicken, salmon, vegetables, or your favorite stir-fry. You can also use it as a dipping sauce.

This Soy-Ginger Glaze adds a delightful balance of sweet, salty, and savory flavors to your dishes. Feel free to adjust the quantities of ingredients to match your taste preferences. Enjoy your homemade glaze!

Homemade BBQ Sauce

Ingredients:

- 1 cup ketchup
- 1/2 cup apple cider vinegar
- 1/4 cup brown sugar
- 2 tablespoons molasses
- 1 tablespoon Dijon mustard
- 1 tablespoon Worcestershire sauce
- 1 teaspoon smoked paprika
- 1 teaspoon garlic powder
- 1/2 teaspoon onion powder
- 1/2 teaspoon black pepper
- 1/2 teaspoon salt
- Optional: hot sauce to taste for some heat

Instructions:

In a medium saucepan, combine ketchup, apple cider vinegar, brown sugar, molasses, Dijon mustard, Worcestershire sauce, smoked paprika, garlic powder, onion powder, black pepper, and salt.
If you like your BBQ sauce with some heat, add hot sauce to taste.
Whisk the ingredients together until well combined.
Place the saucepan over medium heat and bring the mixture to a simmer.
Reduce the heat to low and let the sauce simmer for about 15-20 minutes, stirring occasionally, to allow the flavors to meld and the sauce to thicken.
Taste the BBQ sauce and adjust the seasoning if necessary. If you prefer a sweeter sauce, you can add more brown sugar or molasses.
Once the sauce reaches your desired flavor and consistency, remove it from heat.
Let the Homemade BBQ Sauce cool completely before transferring it to a jar or bottle.

Your Homemade BBQ Sauce is now ready to be used on grilled meats, burgers, pulled pork, or any other dishes you desire. Enjoy the rich, homemade flavor!

Teriyaki Glaze

Ingredients:

- 1/2 cup soy sauce
- 1/4 cup mirin (Japanese sweet rice wine)
- 2 tablespoons sake (or white wine)
- 3 tablespoons brown sugar
- 1 tablespoon honey
- 2 cloves garlic, minced
- 1 teaspoon fresh ginger, grated
- 1 tablespoon cornstarch (optional, for thickening)

Instructions:

In a small saucepan, combine soy sauce, mirin, sake, brown sugar, honey, minced garlic, and grated ginger.

Whisk the ingredients together over medium heat until the sugar has dissolved.

Bring the mixture to a simmer and let it cook for about 8-10 minutes, allowing the flavors to meld and the sauce to slightly thicken.

If you prefer a thicker glaze, mix 1 tablespoon of cornstarch with 2 tablespoons of water to create a slurry. Add the slurry to the sauce and stir continuously until it thickens.

Once the Teriyaki Glaze reaches your desired consistency, remove it from heat.

Allow the glaze to cool slightly before using it. It will continue to thicken as it cools.

Use the Teriyaki Glaze as a marinade for chicken, beef, or vegetables, or brush it on grilled or roasted dishes for a flavorful finish.

Store any leftover Teriyaki Glaze in a sealed container in the refrigerator for future use.

Enjoy your homemade Teriyaki Glaze on a variety of dishes!

Homemade Enchilada Sauce

Ingredients:

- 2 tablespoons vegetable oil
- 2 tablespoons all-purpose flour
- 4 tablespoons chili powder
- 1/2 teaspoon ground cumin
- 1/4 teaspoon garlic powder
- 1/4 teaspoon onion powder
- 1/4 teaspoon dried oregano
- 2 cups vegetable or chicken broth
- 1 can (8 ounces) tomato sauce
- 1 teaspoon sugar
- Salt and pepper to taste

Instructions:

In a medium saucepan, heat the vegetable oil over medium heat.
Stir in the flour and continue to stir for about 1-2 minutes to make a roux.
Add the chili powder, cumin, garlic powder, onion powder, and dried oregano. Stir well to combine.
Gradually whisk in the vegetable or chicken broth to avoid lumps. Continue whisking until the mixture is smooth.
Stir in the tomato sauce and sugar. Mix well.
Bring the mixture to a simmer and let it cook for about 10-15 minutes, stirring occasionally, until the enchilada sauce thickens.
Season the sauce with salt and pepper to taste.
Once the sauce has reached your desired consistency, remove it from heat.
Allow the Enchilada Sauce to cool slightly before using it in your favorite enchilada recipe.
Store any leftover sauce in a sealed container in the refrigerator.

Now you have a delicious and homemade Enchilada Sauce ready to elevate your enchiladas or other Mexican dishes!

Sun-Dried Tomato Pesto

Ingredients:

- 1 cup sun-dried tomatoes (dry-packed, not in oil)
- 2 cloves garlic, peeled
- 1/2 cup fresh basil leaves
- 1/4 cup pine nuts
- 1/2 cup grated Parmesan cheese
- 1/2 cup extra-virgin olive oil
- Salt and pepper to taste

Instructions:

If your sun-dried tomatoes are not packed in oil, rehydrate them by placing them in a bowl of hot water for about 10-15 minutes. Drain and pat them dry.
In a food processor, combine the sun-dried tomatoes, garlic, basil, pine nuts, and Parmesan cheese.
Pulse the ingredients a few times to break them down.
While the food processor is running, slowly drizzle in the olive oil until the mixture comes together into a smooth paste.
Stop the food processor and scrape down the sides with a spatula. Taste and adjust the seasoning with salt and pepper as needed.
Continue processing until the Sun-Dried Tomato Pesto reaches your desired consistency. If it's too thick, you can add a bit more olive oil.
Once the pesto is well blended, transfer it to a jar or airtight container.
Store the Sun-Dried Tomato Pesto in the refrigerator. It can be used immediately or kept for a week or two.

This Sun-Dried Tomato Pesto is perfect for tossing with pasta, spreading on sandwiches, or using as a flavorful topping for grilled meats and vegetables. Enjoy!

www.ingramcontent.com/pod-product-compliance
Lightning Source LLC
LaVergne TN
LVHW061949070526
838199LV00060B/4044